Stephen and David Isaacs, who wrote this book, are twins. The picture above shows both of them, along with their nanny and their dog, Linda.

Stephen and David are both children's doctors. David is a paediatrician in Sydney. He is a vocal advocate for child refugees. Meanwhile, Stephen is a child psychiatrist who lives in London. He made all the illustrations in this book.

29.10.2020

To Aaron

Hope you enjoy this Marsupial & Monotremes book

With best wishes

Steve

(Echidna)

OUCH in the POUCH

Musical Marsupials and Monotremes

Stephen and David Isaacs

Austin Macauley Publishers™
LONDON • CAMBRIDGE • NEW YORK • SHARJAH

Copyright © Stephen and David Isaacs (2020)

The right of Stephen and David Isaacs to be identified as authors of this work has been asserted by the authors in accordance with section 77 and 78 of the Copyright, Designs and Patents Act 1988.

All rights reserved. No part of this publication may be reproduced, stored in a retrieval system, or transmitted in any form or by any means, electronic, mechanical, photocopying, recording, or otherwise, without the prior permission of the publishers.

Any person who commits any unauthorised act in relation to this publication may be liable to criminal prosecution and civil claims for damages.

This is a work of fiction. Names, characters, businesses, places, events, locales, and incidents are either the products of the author's imagination or used in a fictitious manner. Any resemblance to actual persons, living or dead, or actual events is purely coincidental.

A CIP catalogue record for this title is available from the British Library.

ISBN 9781528994385 (Paperback)
ISBN 9781528994392 (ePub e-book)

www.austinmacauley.com

First Published (2020)
Austin Macauley Publishers Ltd
25 Canada Square
Canary Wharf
London
E14 5LQ

Dedicated to our sister, Harriet, and our grandchildren, Charlie, Owen, Oliver, Jacob and Zoe.

Thanks to Milena for artistic inspiration.

Synopsis

Parents and grandparents of children aged 3-7 years are the main target audience...but we hope the children will read it too.

How it differs: There are plenty of books about marsupials but none that combine marsupials and music. Monotremes that play music are also hard to find.

Katie is a kangaroo

Who likes to warble on kazoo

In her pouch you'd never know is

A pair of very naughty joeys

Katie never knows what's worst

When they're head or bottom first.

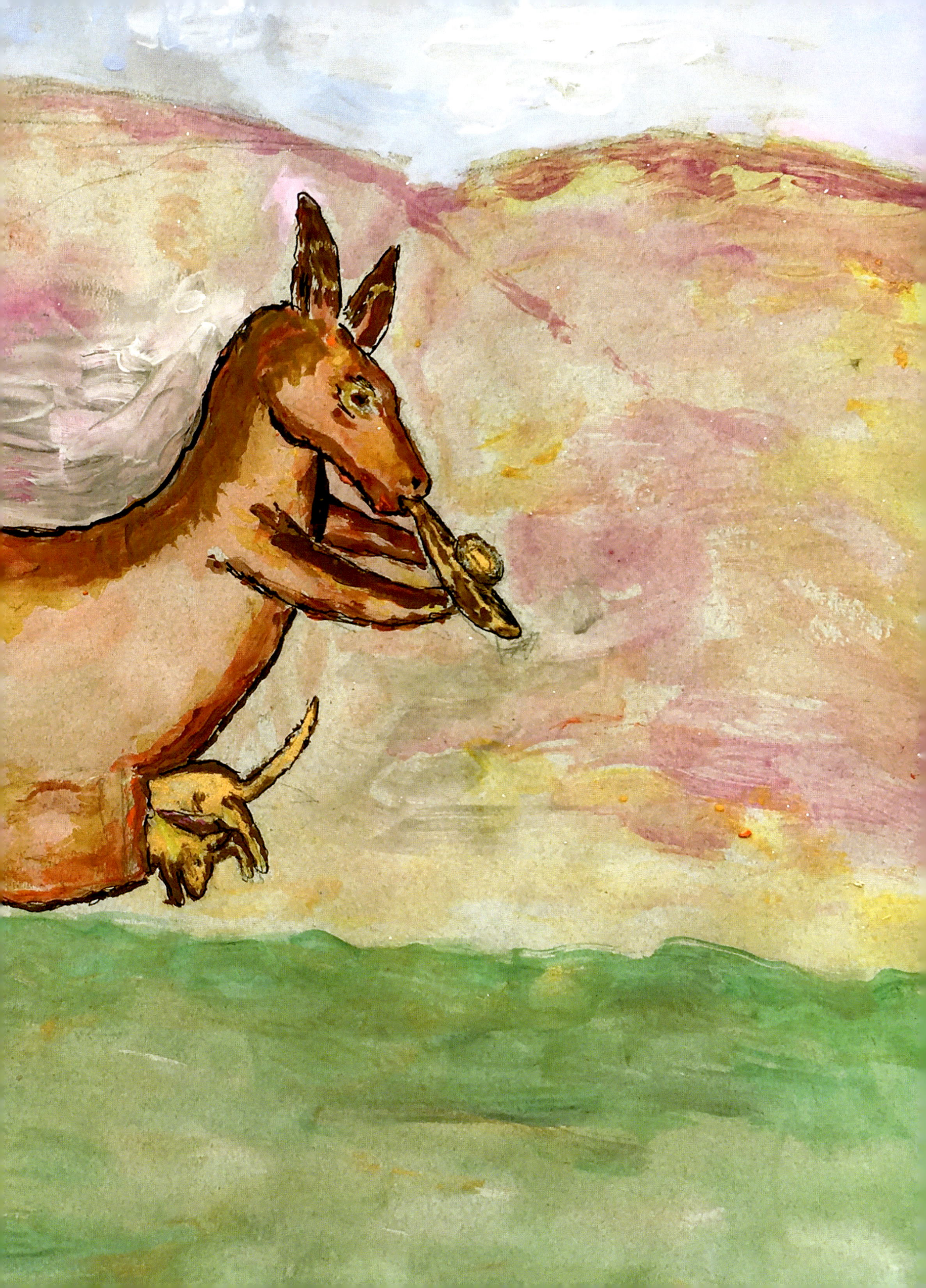

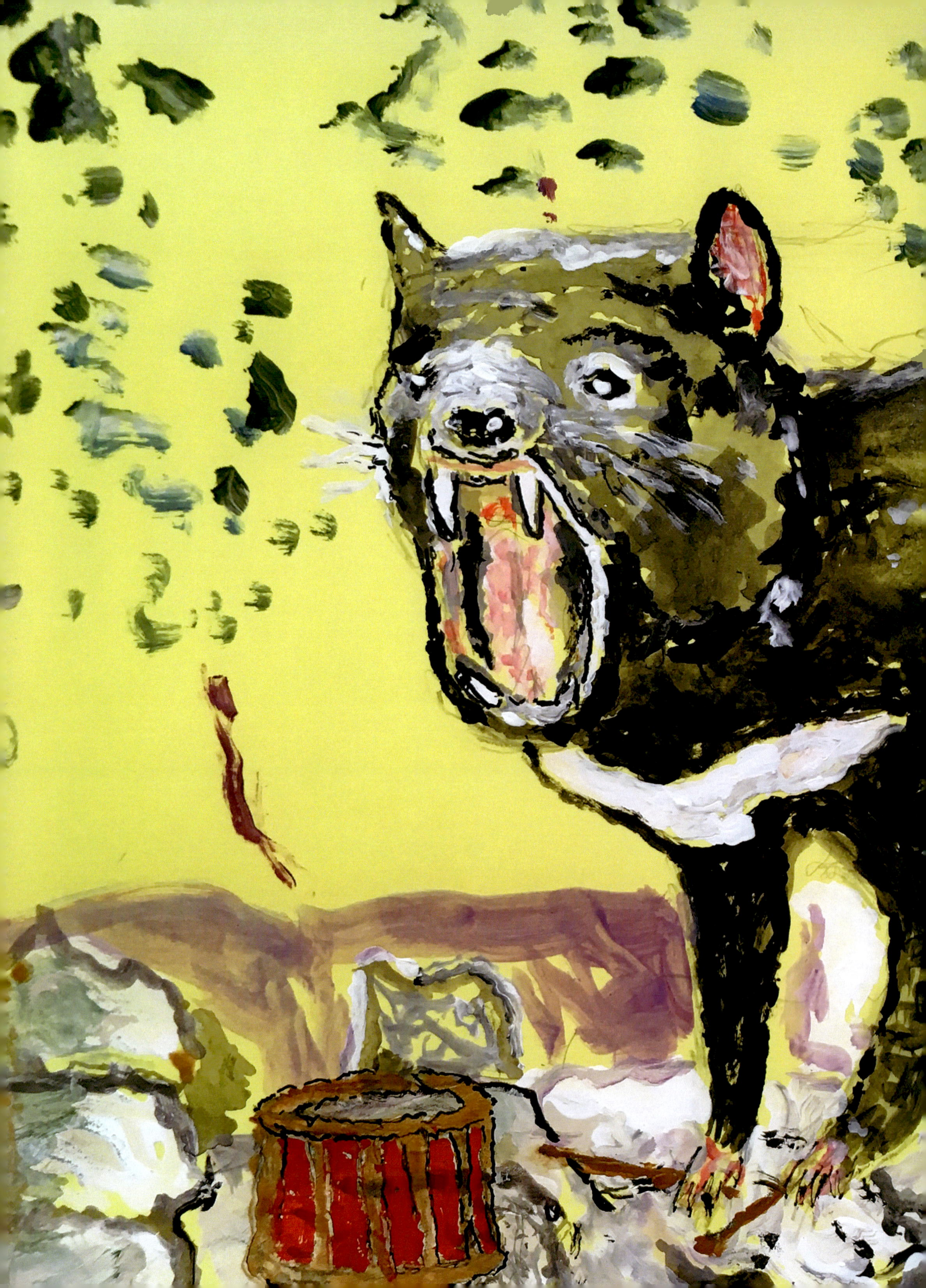

If you prefer deep bass to treble

Please meet Tom Tasmanian Devil

He grunts, he roars,

at night he snores

He fights and then he licks his sores

It's time for bed, the day is done

Tom serenades you on his drum.

Polly Possum's babies blossom

On her back where she can watch them

With her prehensile tail she'll swing

Play guitar and try to sing

But when she sings, she mostly grunts

You would too with slugs for lunch.

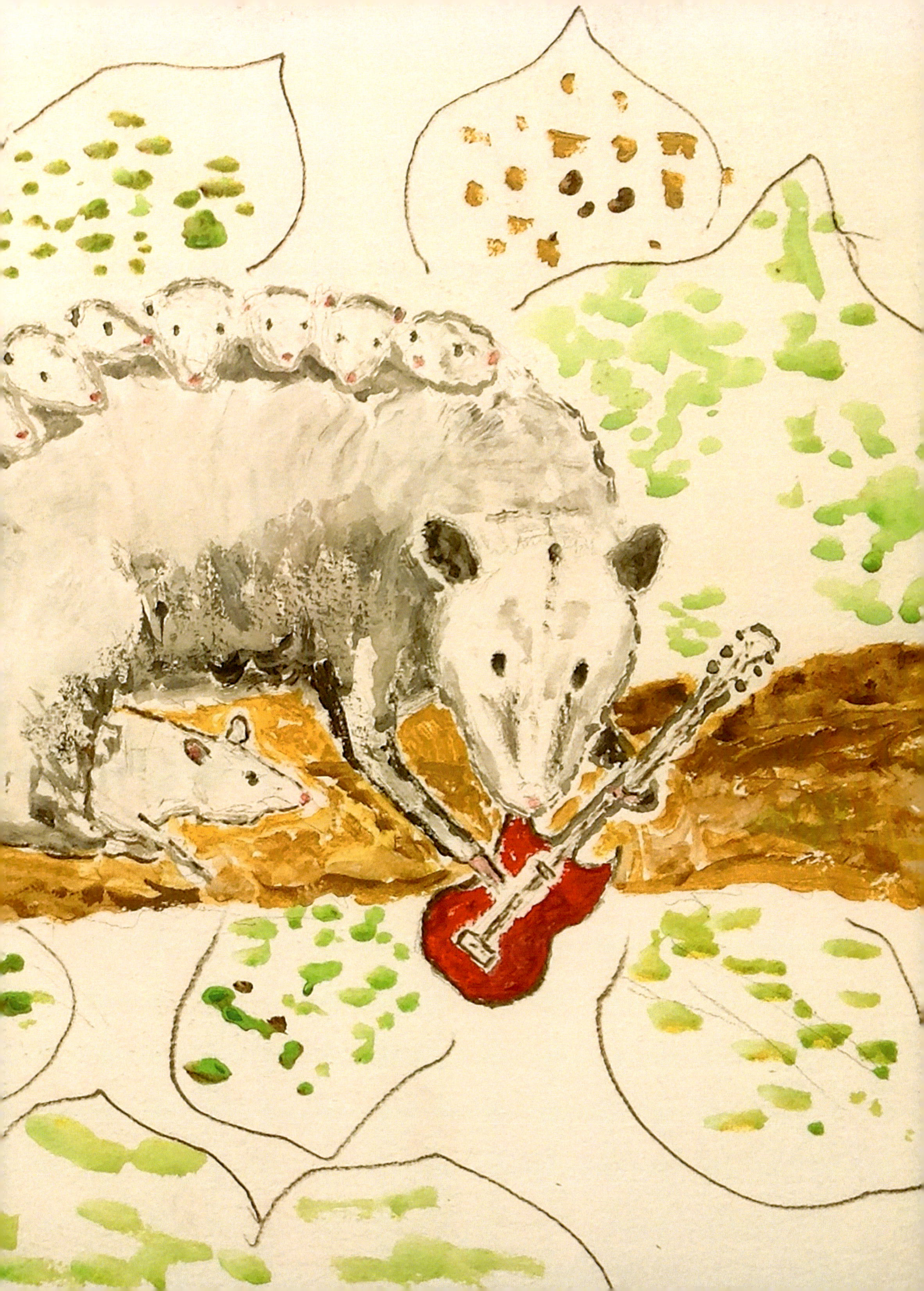

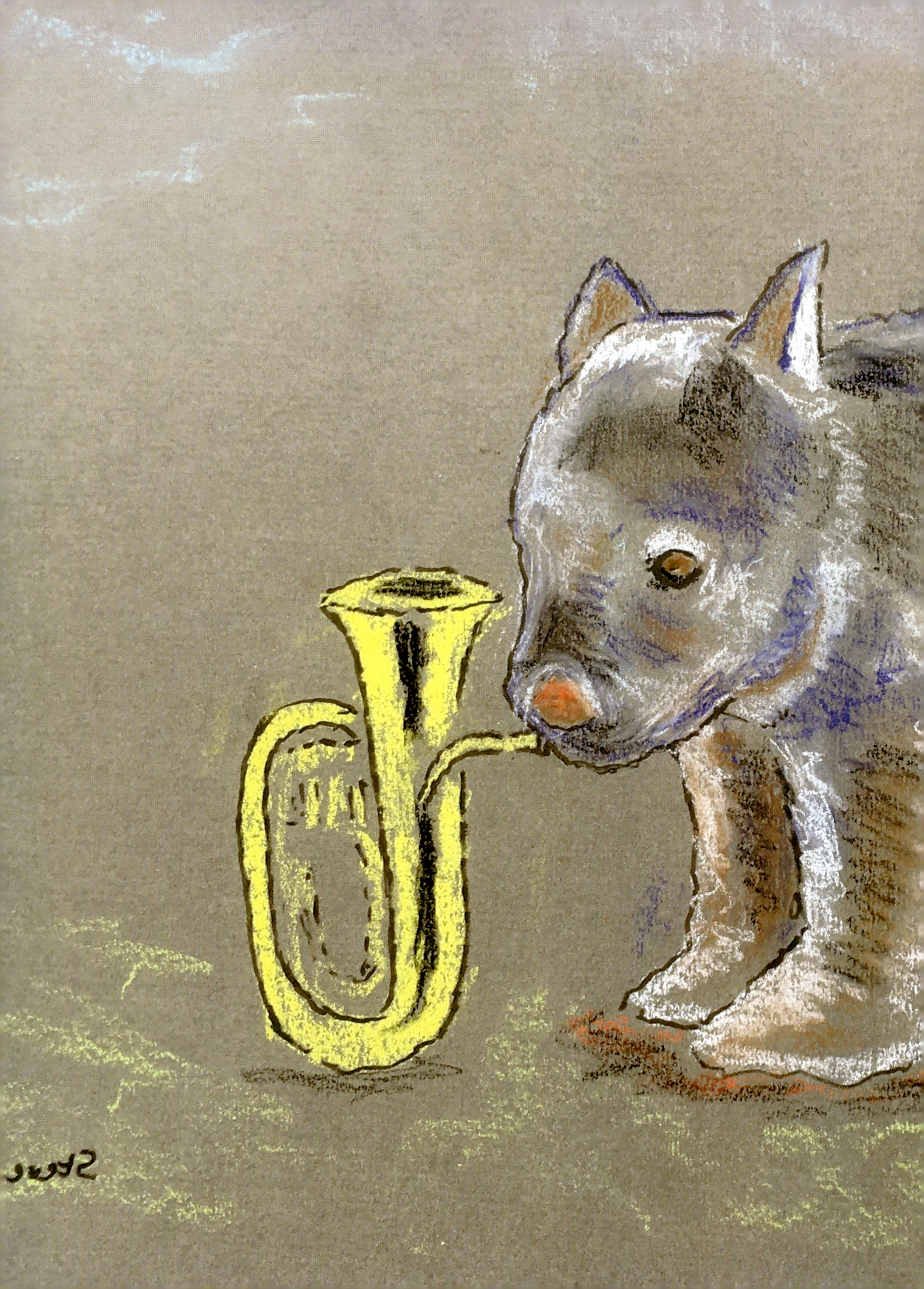

Cubic poo's the way Will Wombat

Avoids the need for unarmed combat

Cubic poo won't roll downhill

Another wombat sniffs the smell

And says "Will Wombat is peculiar

He stinks a bit and plays the tuba."

Catching ants can be quite tricky

So Eve Echidna's tongue is sticky

She has a baby in her pouch

Try to grab her, you'll say ouch

Eve waddles through the bush

while gaily

Playing on the ukulele.

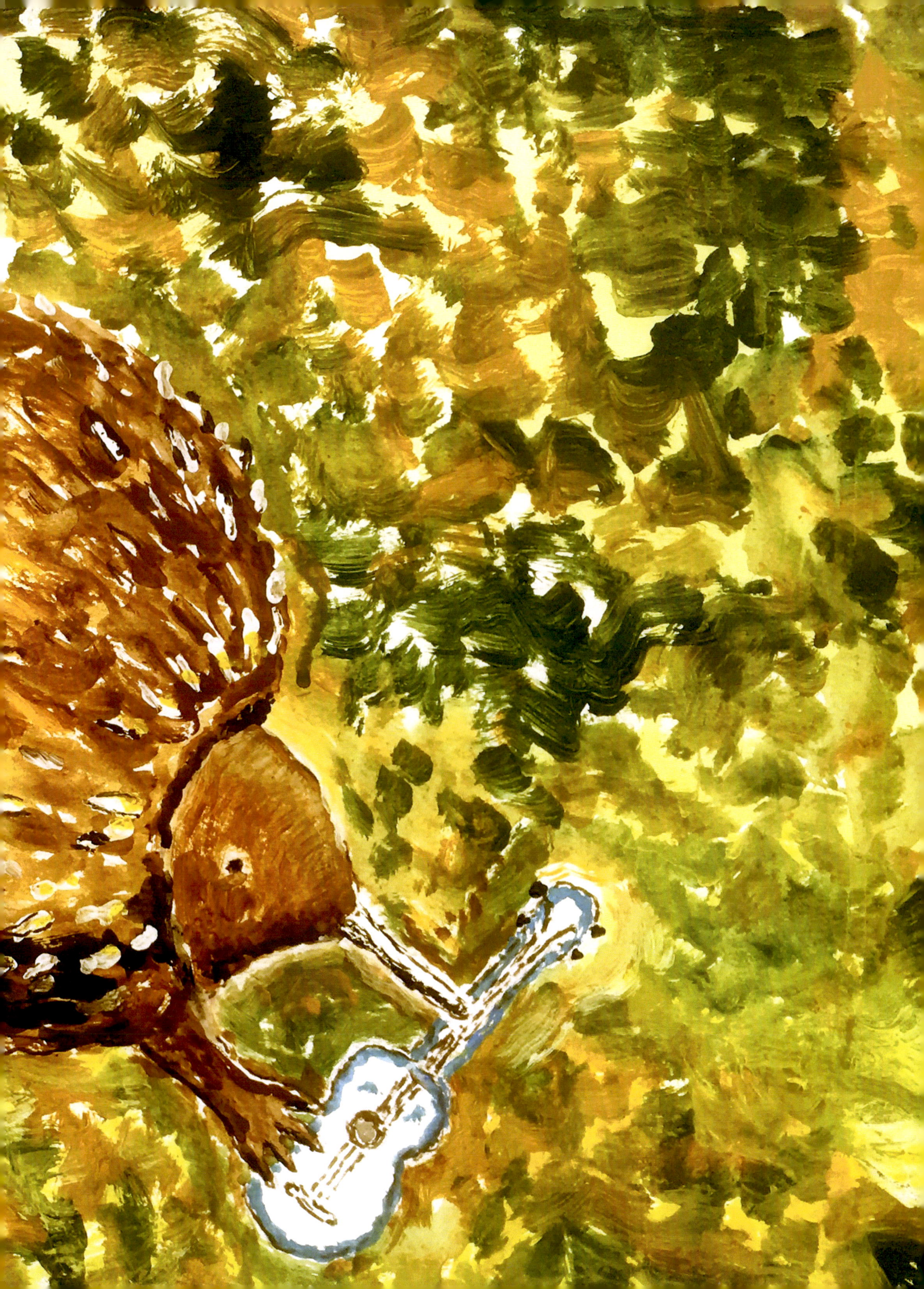

Tasmanian tiger's stripy skin

Was prized by men who hunted him

He tried to slip across the border

Tooting softly on recorder

Alas, before we'd hardly blinked

Tasmanian tiger was extinct.

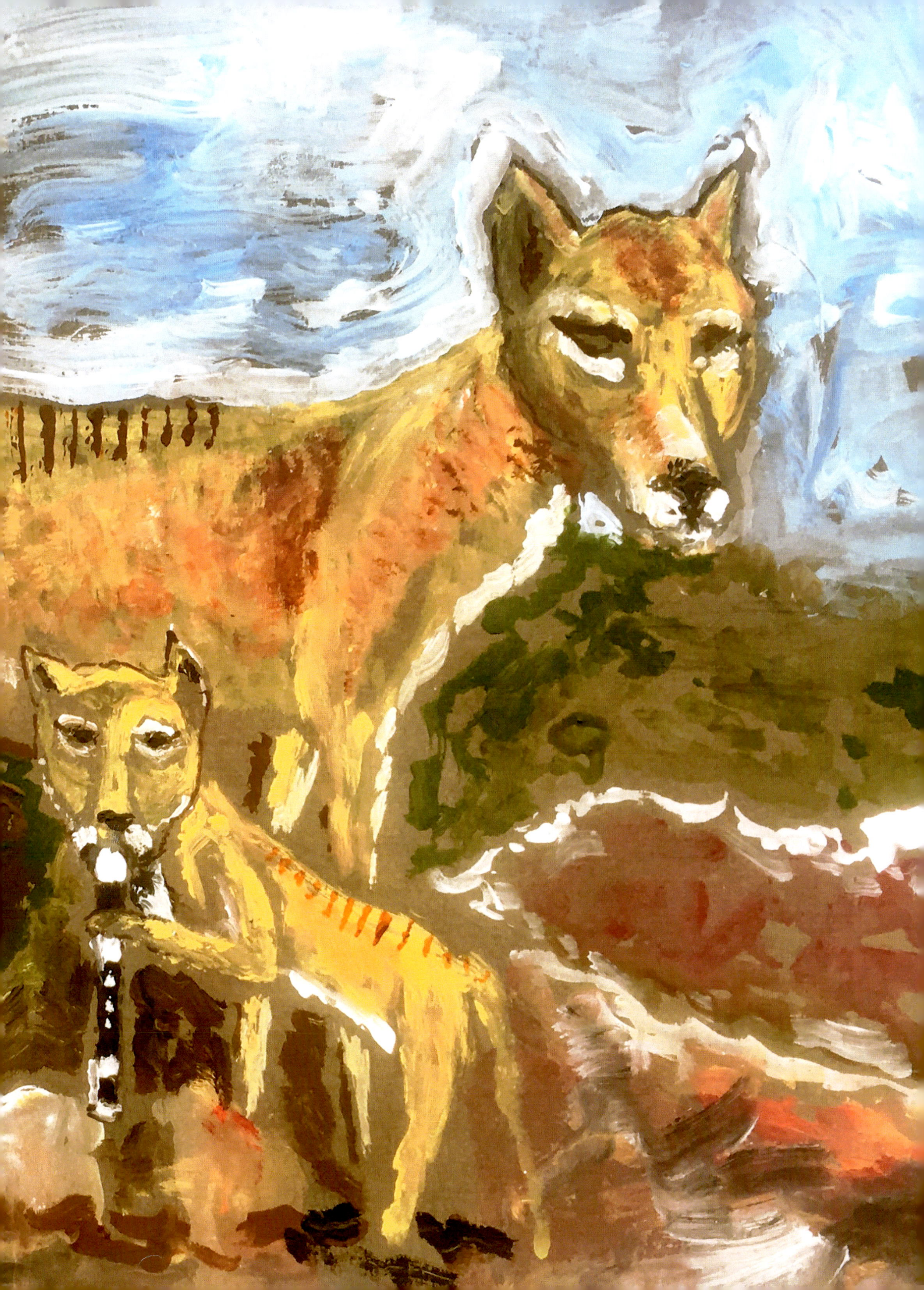

Colin is a cute koala

Snorts in tune with the pianola

If that doesn't win your heart

Colin knows just where to start

He will play for you a solo

Romance on his old viola.

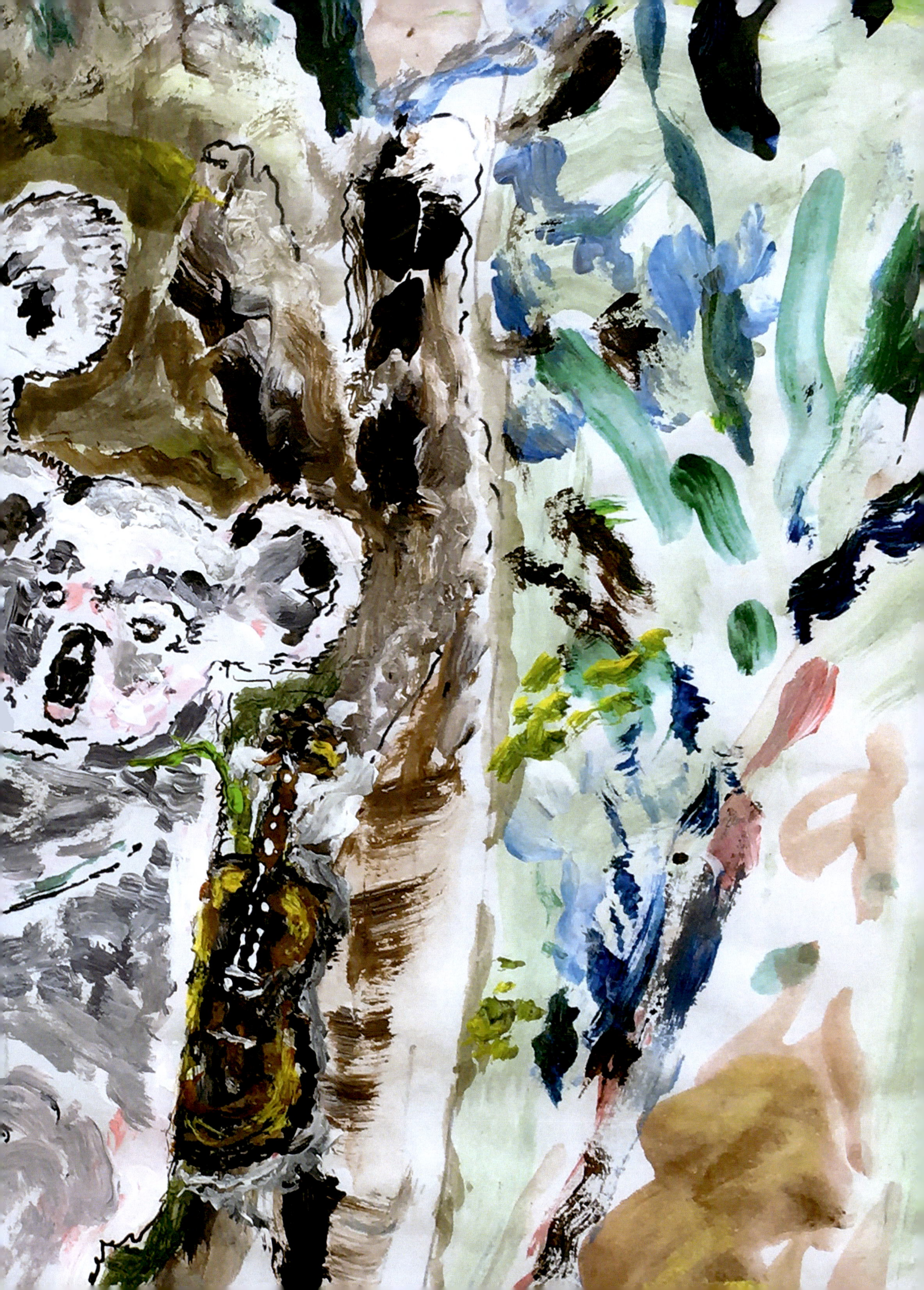

She's quiet, never makes a fuss

Is Patsy-Anne the platypus

She shimmies softly in the water

Lays eggs which hatch to

sons and daughters

When at last it's getting dark

You'll hear her strumming

on the harp.

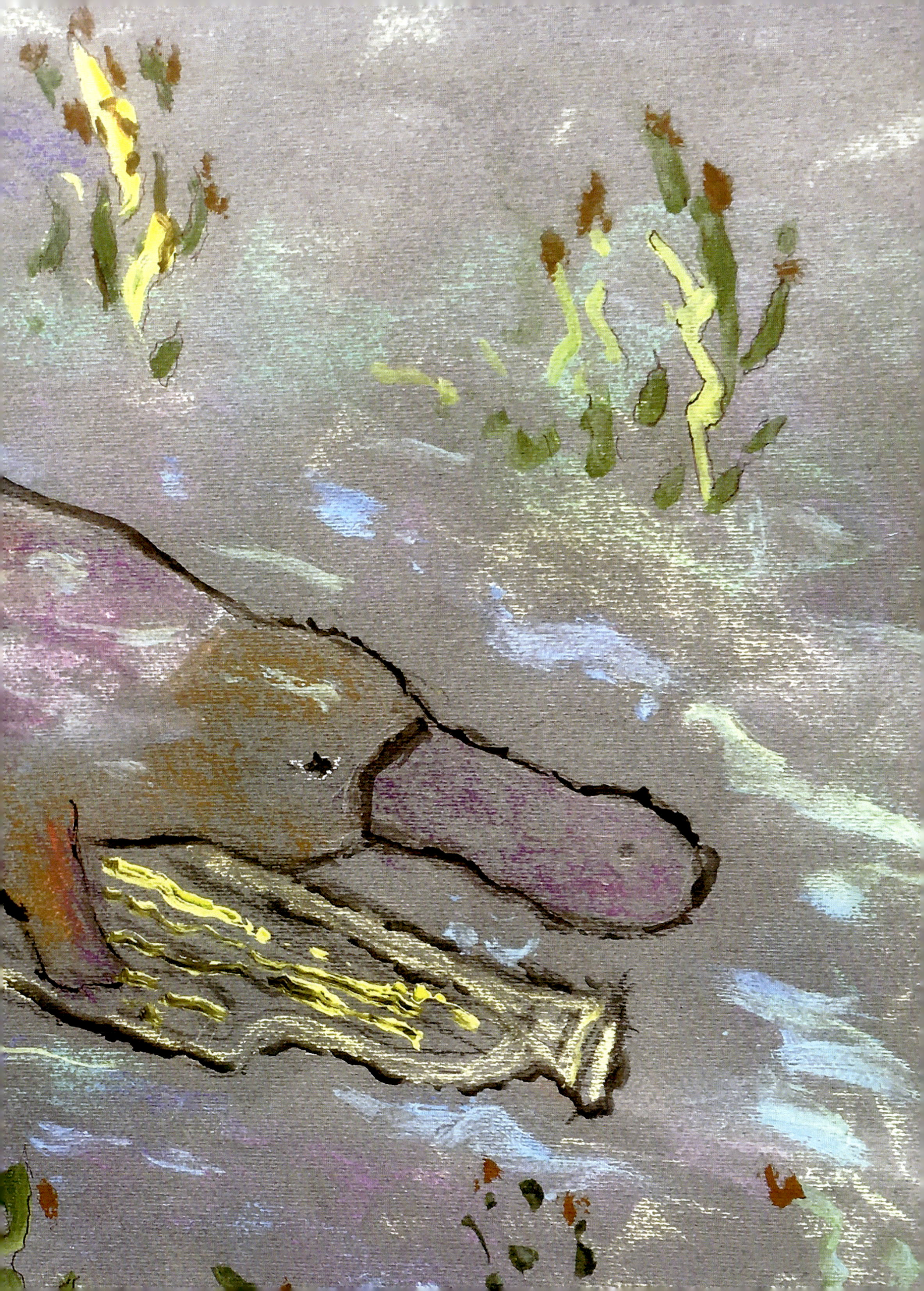

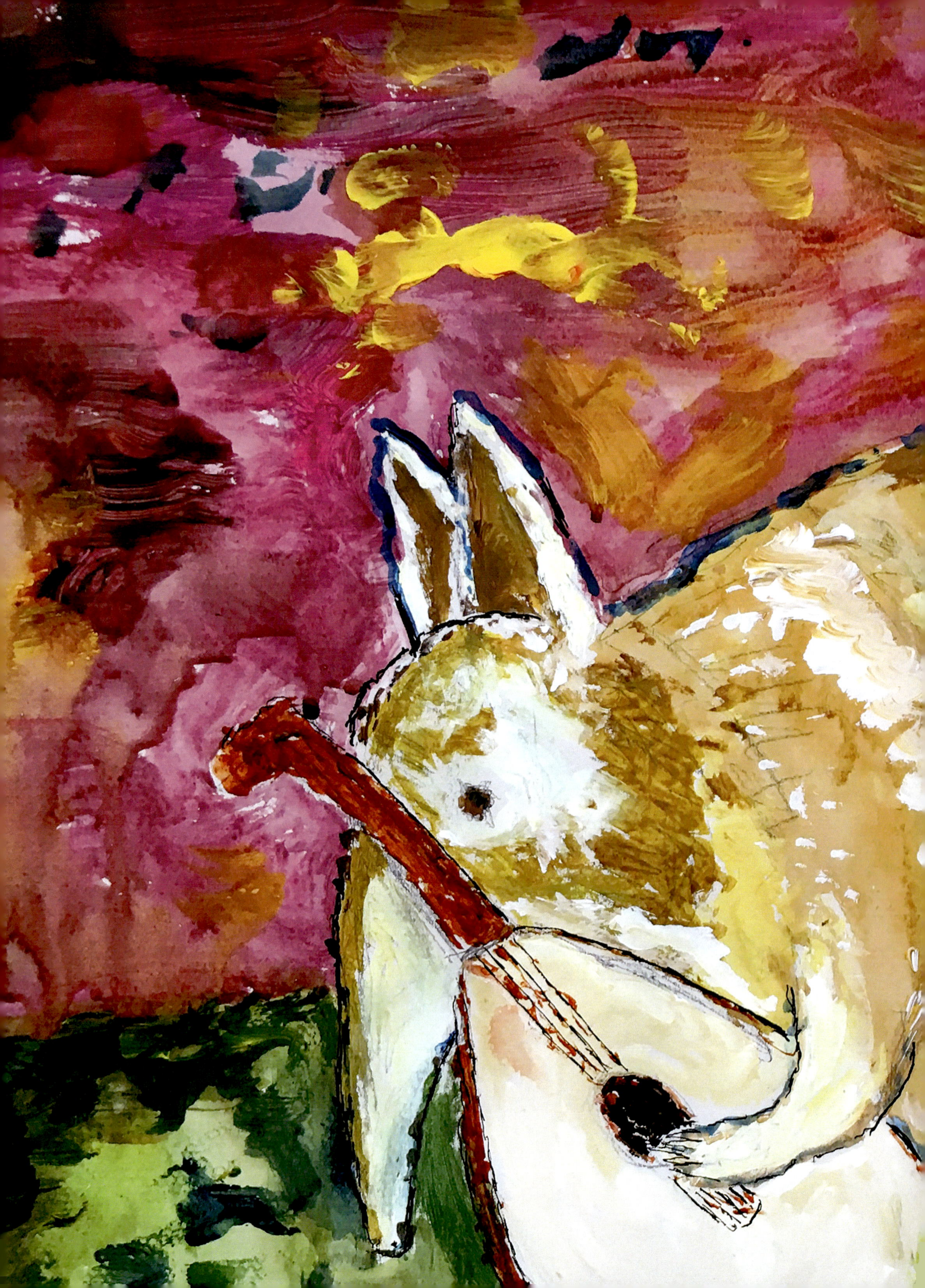

Bob Bandicoot is super cute

Quite dapper in his new zoot suit

He hunts at night, you know what's good

A funnel web's his favourite food

He's very shy Bob Bandicoot

He woos his lady on the lute.

Susie glides from tree to tree

She does it oh so gracefully

Surprise, surprise, though, sugar glider

Sips nectar, likes to eat a spider

She'll crunch a beetle, munch an egg

Tinkle a xylophone with her leg.

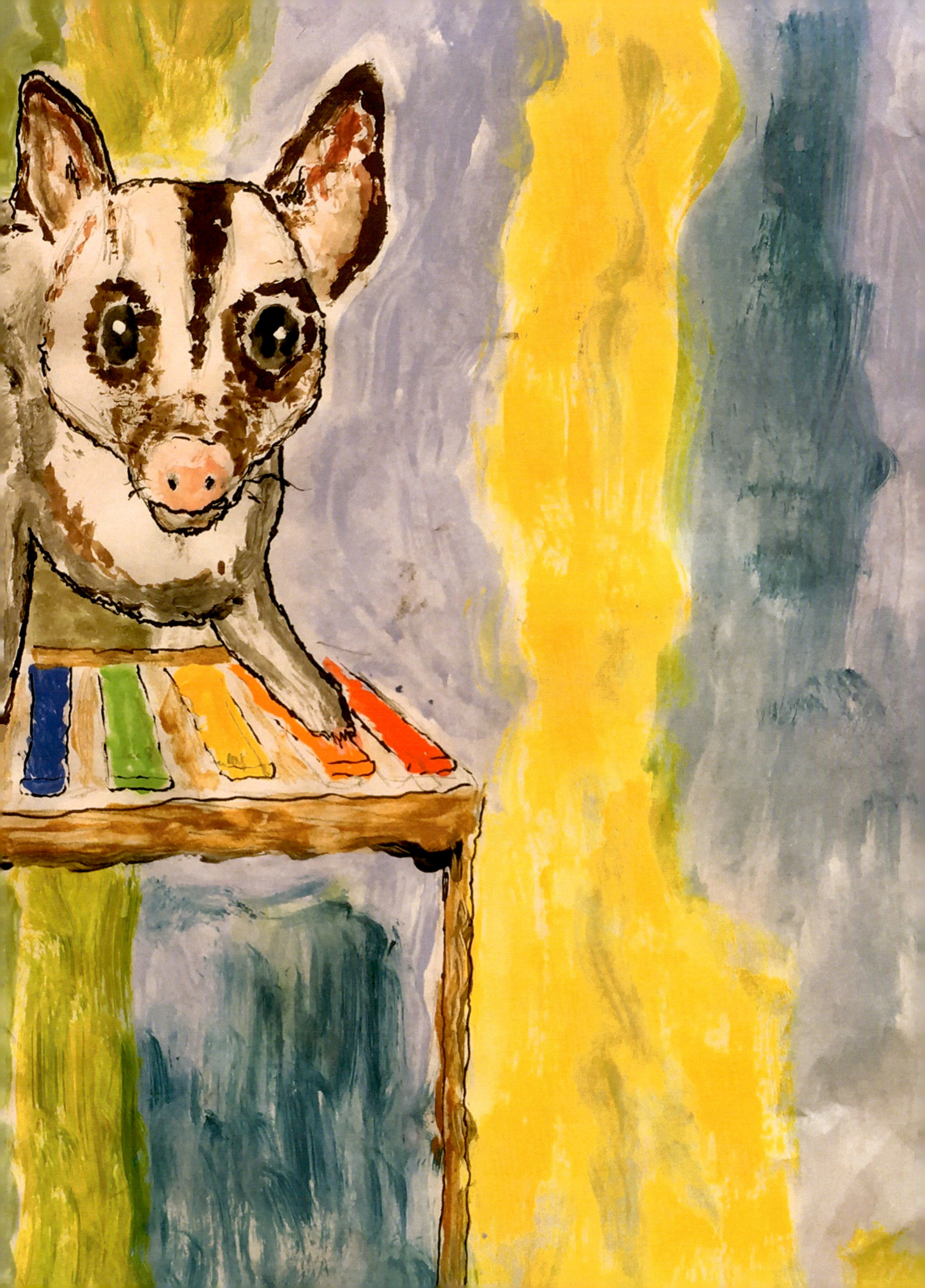

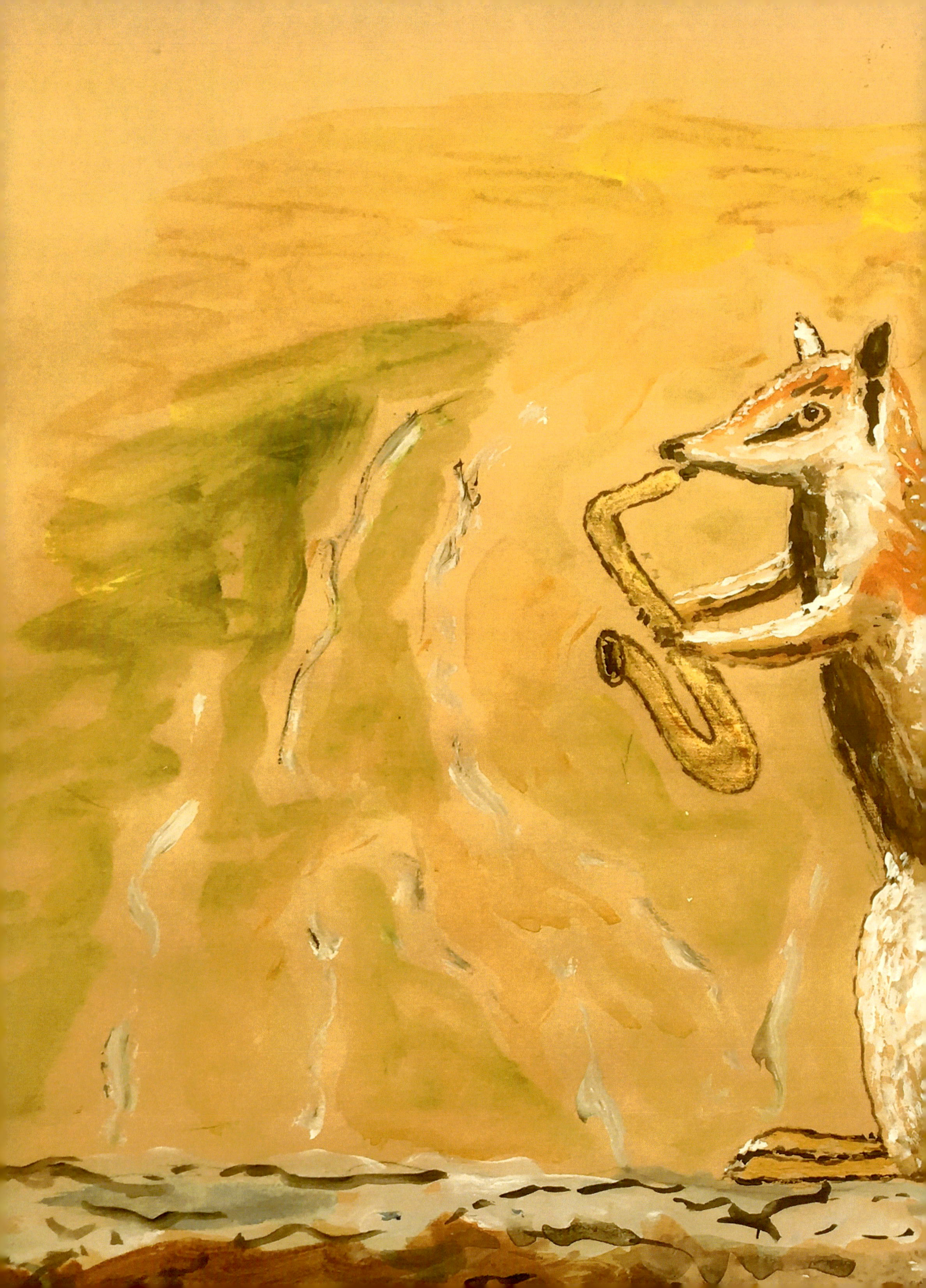

This numbat by the name of Neville

Plays saxophone, he's one cool devil

Juicy ants there's nothing sweeter

He is called the termite-eater

Neville Numbat's not forgotten

You'll know him by his stripy bottom.

Miriam's a marsupial mole

Backwards pouch, so digging a hole

Earth won't fill up Miriam's pouch

And dirt won't clog up baby's mouth

Mum kicks dirt from the hole

to dump it

Playing a fanfare on her trumpet.

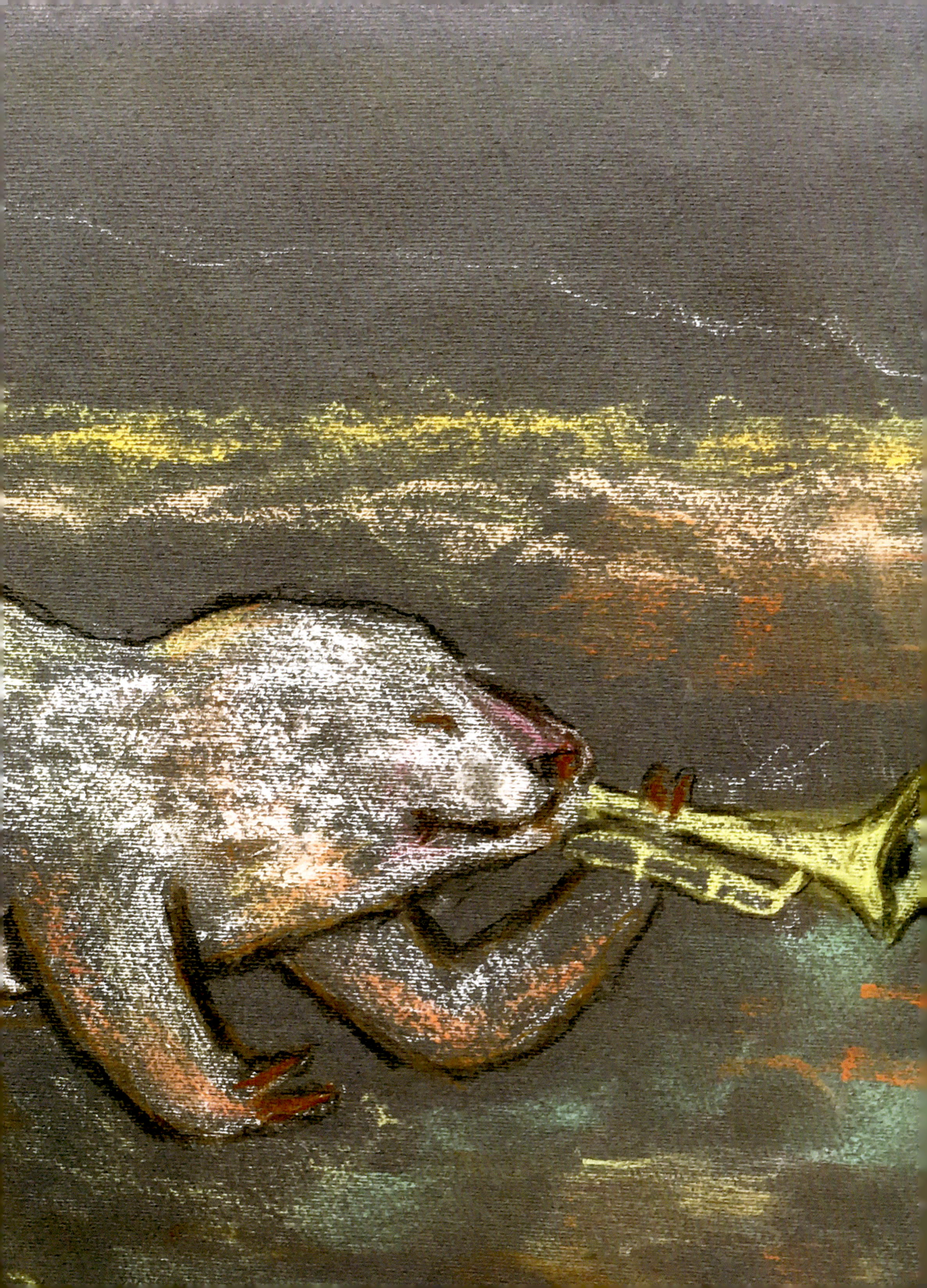

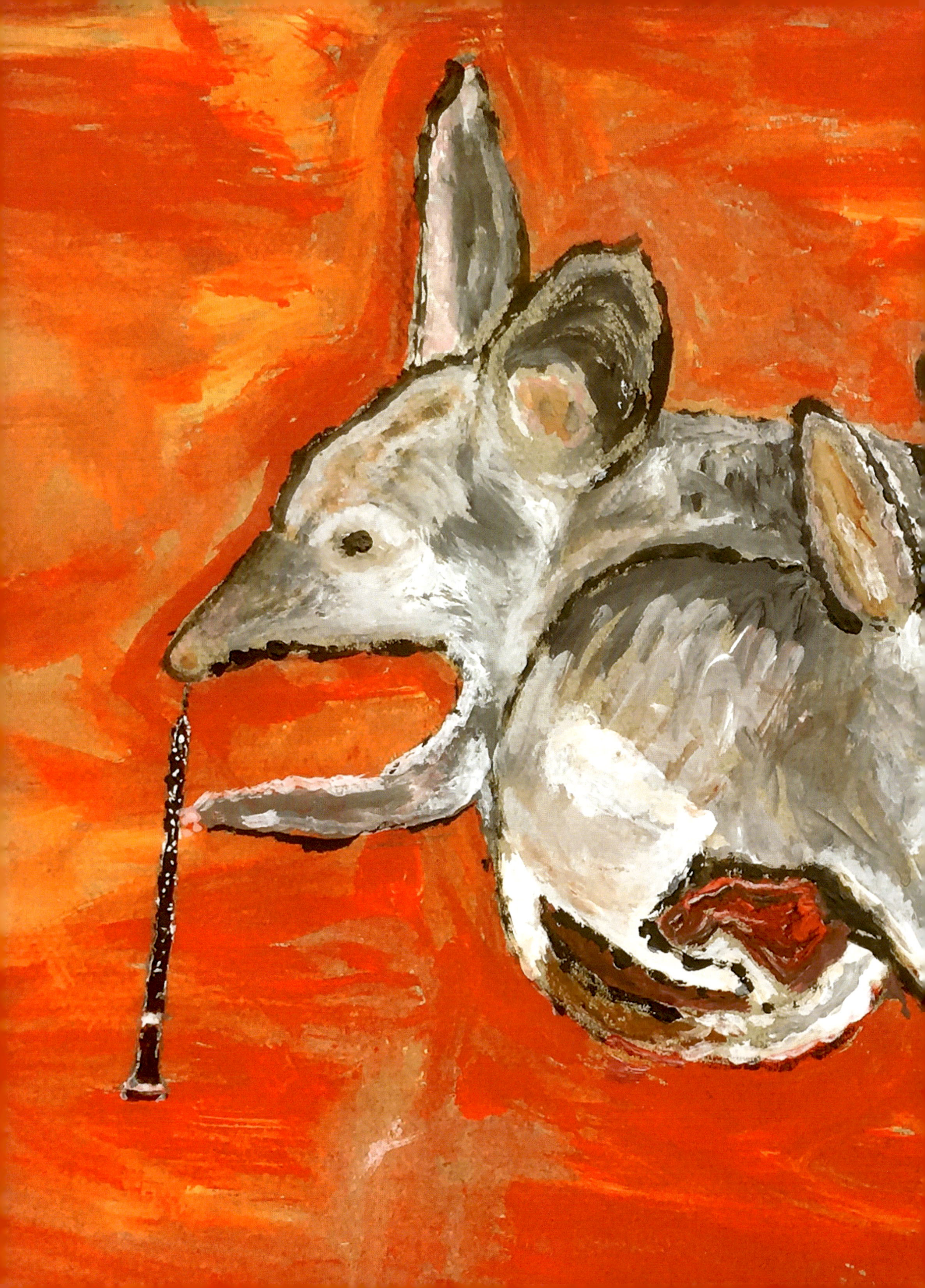

Billy Bilby has big ears

They keep him cool,

they help him hear

When hunting insects in the night

His pointy nose is quite a sight

A burrow is his bed by day

The oboe wails, he sure can play.

Queenie is a quirky quoll

With lots of spots and lots of soul

Her teeth are sharp,

her nose is wet

So when she plays the clarinet

She mustn't chew or slurp too soon

Then she can play a mournful tune.